POEMS FROM
A RENAISSANCE MAN

By Norman Rothfeld

Poems From A Renaissance Man

Copyright © 2023 **Norman Rothfeld**

ALL RIGHTS RESERVED.

Table of Contents

My Legacy, My Gift

I hope that this book of poetry and prose will be my legacy, my gift to my family, friends and future generations.

I will be leaving behind a sample of who I was as a human being, uncovering layer by layer of my identity, while leaving some layers undiscovered.

My legacy is a blueprint, a map exposing the essence of me as a person, perhaps achieving the completion of the canvas of my life here on earth. When I am long gone, this legacy, my stories, my life and life as I viewed it, can live on as a piece of me. People may ask: who was Norm Rothfeld; who was he as a person? My family may ask: who was my father, my grandfather, my great grandfather, my uncle, my cousin? What did he accomplish, how did he view life and his struggles in life as reflected in his writing? What was beneath the persona of his presentation in the world? How was his character, his humor, his sadness, his compassion for others described?

It is said that a picture is worth a thousand words. An authored book as a legacy is priceless.

I want to dedicate this book to my loving wife Barbara who has been a supportive listener and life partner and has kept me centered as a calming influence for me. She kept her own identity, as I kept mine. Barbara was always there through thick or thin, the good and bad, a beacon for my ship finding its way in the sea of uncertainty and self-doubt.

I also wish to dedicate this book to my friend Dr. Michael Parish, who has for the last 12 years motivated me and offered guidance on my wavering road to self-discovery. He has provided insight into how I can express my own truth, while overcoming the fears I had to fully develop my creative abilities. Dr. Parish discovered early on that I was "A Renaissance Man." I thank him for that.

Norm Rothfeld

About the Author

My business career involved owning a garment import company for many years and then working for a car company before retiring two years ago. I have been married for over 40 years and have two daughters and two granddaughters. We lived on the Upper West side of Manhattan near Lincoln Center for many years and then moved to Scarsdale, New York. We now own a condominium in Kings Point, Tamarac FL, near Fort Lauderdale. I attended Hunter and City College in NYC.

I have been writing poetry and prose since I was 17 years old. I stopped writing for many years, beginning again about 10 years ago, at age 72, when my observation and interpretation of life took on a new meaning. I was eager to share my writing with others.

I am passionate to end homelessness in Broward County FL, writing about the homeless and volunteering at numerous local charitable organizations.

I am a member of the Veterans Advisory board of Sunrise FL, working to improve the lives of veterans with available healthcare and other benefits. I enjoy getting involved in local community activities.

I have been called 'A Renaissance Man' probably because I enjoy many different subjects to explore and discuss with people. I enjoy philosophy, psychology, theology and history. I like to listen to others and discuss the various opinions and thoughts about most subjects. Maybe my writing is sourced from my desire for knowledge of these many subjects.

Where does creativity come from? For me, writing comes from my heart and soul, and from my life. My passion for life's beauty demands a way for me to express myself. Writing is one form that supports my fulfilling that self-expression. I am proud to have been a nominee for the Florida State Poet laureate in 2020.

Creative writing doesn't necessarily require a college degree. One can learn the technique of writing in a classroom. The essence of writing also comes from another deeper heartfelt place, not always found in the classroom.

If any person receives pleasure from reading anything I write, that's rewarding to me.

Like a beautiful mockingbird nesting in my heart and yearning to sing and take flight, the words within me must also sing out and take flight.

Life then becomes more exhilarating and so freeing.

Norm Rothfeld.

Prologue

Many of us experience an incident that impacts our life.

Sometimes we don't realize in that moment what the impact is or will be.

It can be an "aha"" moment, occurring years later, that brings forth the memory of that incident. That's what occurred for me.

A tragedy occurred in 1957 that dramatically affected my life.

My uncle George, my mother's only brother and beloved by the entire family, died from a massive heart attack in his wife Gerry's arms. He was only 48 years old. I was stunned when I heard the news. I was 17 years old at the time and his death was the first shocking loss that I experienced. It was a surreal moment for everyone attending the funeral.

I remember being upset and confused, not knowing how to handle his death.

I began to write these first 23 poems over the next year or so, bringing forth the emotion and hurt that was suppressed, crying to emerge. The poems were a catharsis to begin the healing process, expressing my feelings.

I didn't realize or understand how I knew to write about seemingly grown-up themes of life and love and abstract thoughts. My "aha" moment of genesis came a few years ago after reading and rereading the poems.

I realized that I was writing about my aunt and uncle, sharing with others their unrequited love and passion for each other.

I now understand the motivation for, and the meaning of these early poems mostly written 59 years ago.

I hope that you find these poems worthwhile and thought provoking.

Perhaps these poems will elicit your "aha" moment.

Thank you,

Norm

2016

LOVE

All Together

The man searched for years

Oh, so many wretched years

Seeking what he knew already

Hoping what he hoped all along

He hoped to find happiness

He sought riches and glory

And he was ready to die

All those years wasted

Around him stood his children and wife

He looked out passed them all

Seeing the sun rising above

Casting a halo around his family

Then, only then did he realize

All his searching was in vain

All those years were in waste

For his happiness stood around him

There all those years

As his eyes gently closed

His family noticed something

A smile at his lips

Rolling tears, glowing from the radiant sun

At his eyes

The man had found his happiness.

The Time Sure Goes

Oh, how the years pass so quickly

Only memories now

But they were good years

The time sure goes

And, now we're old

Our hair is thin and gray

Our old suits fit no more

The time sure goes

The children

Oh, the troubles, worries

Were they worth it? Certainly

The time sure goes

I never thought we would get by

We fooled them all; we showed them

You and l, we showed the world

The time sure goes

The bad with the good

We had a little of both

But we had good times,

only memories now

But they were good years

You and I, always together

The two of us made good of bad

The time sure goes

But the memories are fresh

They alone will be our life, our hope

For with them, all our troubles, all our pain

Will have been worthwhile

But remember, darling,

My life would have been so empty

If I had not you

The time sure goes.

Tell Me, Please, What Is Love?

Tell me, please, what is love?

Is it something real or something not

Do I find it anyplace, or must I travel far

If I turn around, will love be there

And if I hope, will love be near

Is love something which I may fear

Or is it something which holds dear

And if I find love, will it stay

Or will love just turn another way

And how can I tell if love comes to me

By a kiss, or by a sigh or by a sweet hello

Will love come up to me and say, "here I am"

"Take me; I am what you are searching for"

Look no more fool, look no more

Search no more, have no more strife

You've been married to love all your life.

The Dream You Are

True my love, there have been others

But the others were not you

Sincerity is a word I have just learned

Only now can I say I love you

To you my darling, to you

You my love, are beautiful

Others too have beauty

But my love, you possess something

Which no other can claim

When my love, I am thinking of you

No other thoughts enter into my mind

When my love, you are near to me

The closeness of you fulfills my desires

When my love, I wonder

Why is all this so?

I think because

That's the dream you are

When I am alone you are with me

The thought brings you closer

Closer to my mind and my heart

And my loneliness ceases

Soon my darling, I am in a great room

There is music, dancing and joviality

Soon my love, I am alone with you

Near, so near holding you

At any moment I can think of this

Effortless, without any care or pain

No more do I worry about finding you

Thank you so much my darling

For being the dream you are.

Our Love

Once in a while love may stray

But our love dearest is here to stay

Our love will keep for all eternity

No matter what will come, God almighty

Our youth will endure forever and ever

Heartache in life I pray will come never

Though the faces of others my turn and yearn

Our love dearest will heat and burn

On and on for all to see

And wonder why

They can't be you and me.

There Are Times

There are times, I guess

When so little is offered

So little is gained

But then I guess that was when I had not you

There are times I guess

When the brightest day

Is the darkest night

When the sky hovers down

Blanketing my soul

But then I guess

That was when I had not you.

No Matter What

No matter what the times may bring

As long as I hear the Robins sing

Come whatever, I don't care

As long as I have you my dear

Let the earth's crust burst open

Let the sea's body pour forth

I don't care, I don't care

As long as I have you my dear.

As The Day Goes By

As the day goes by, dear

One more day that we've had

To be together - to live together

To pass the time away

Eternity could not be long enough

To let our love persist

Say that you will always be near

To share my love - to give me love

Forever, never to part.

One

Beauty, come once more to me as before

Whisper in my ear, linger at my side

Stay; oh, stay not forever, if only for a moment

The two of us are one

Molded and unbroken

Together, we will be forever

Beauty, come once more to me as before.

Into Each Life

Into each life comes what may
Some sadness, some trouble, a ray
Of happiness
Search all you wish, hope and pray
And then, you too, one day
Will see that into your life
Will come what may
Some sadness, some trouble, a ray
Of happiness.

When I Sit Down And Think

When I sit down and think

Of the things I've done

And the things I will do

I say to myself, life is so short

How can I do all the things I want?

When I sit down and think

What if I don't do all that I want

Will the world be missing something?

Will the world get over its loss?

Of course it will, I hope it will

And what will happen when I die

Will I be mourned?

And what if I'm not

Will it be so bad?

Of course not

So, if I will not be mourned

If I won't do all the things I want

If the world won't miss me

What will be the sense of trying?

Try hell, I'm going to sleep

Oh, Sheltered Flower

Emerge, oh sheltered flower

Rise up and greet the day

You were always so friendly

Now, when everything is alive

You stay hidden

Are you fearful of what is to come?

Be not fearful of the unknown

The sun will protect you

The moisture will bathe you

You shall live.

Sheltered

Sheltered for many months, the trees finally emerge

From there embodiment, and blossom

The flowers, useless and daunt, become alive with color

The trees are free

The flowers are free

Everything is free.

The Sea Cries Out

The sea wondrous, cries out

Like a magnificent hand, clutching and rolling

The waves call me, they do

From near and far they call me, crying out

Reach for me, pull for me

And I go, for I must

As if in a trance, I wander and yet I know

For the waves call me, they do

And I listen and I go.

When I Saw The Light

I saw the light, there was darkness

When I heard the sound, there was silence

The beginning becomes the end

The group is one

The light is behind us

The sound is softly in the past

What is the future, but the past?

Who are we? Who am I?

But light, sound, future and past

The day and night are no longer seen

Where is everything?

I can only see the past

And hope for the future.

I'm a Hero From The West

I'm a hero from the west

I fought the Indians to the test

When the cavalry gave up

To the fight I did gallop

I'm a hero from the west

All the girls like me best

They all compete to no avail

For it's my horse that I do trail

I cannot help it, what the hell

I'm a hero from the west

The marshals in the town all yell for me

When I come to help, they jump for glee

Once the bad men hear, they do run

I guess it's because of my gun

I'm a hero from the west

Taking into account all that I've done

I can rightly say it's all been fun

But W-H-E-R-E'-S the bath? - I've had none

I'm a hero from the west.

If I Had A Chance

If I had a chance to live and see

All the things those are dear to me

I would not ask for all the riches

They are not for me

I ask only for the simple things

To have the sun and the moon above

To be able to have your love

To clutch the soil of the earth

To feel the wind, the rain and seed

Having your love is all I need.

I Was In Shadow, I Was

I was in shadow, I was

Night was low, day was sung

Together the pair of us did walk

Holding together

At the end of our walk daylight stood

Magnificent, true, bright and clear

And I did sing

There I did gaze in wonderment

Depression and sorrow no more

For at the end of our walk where daylight stood

Was you.

Enter Into The City

Enter into the city

A magnificent array of molded stone

Thought of as harsh, loud and dark

But seen as bright, soft and wonderful

Man to beauty, seen and loved

It is not what is seen that is so wonderful

The mirror of life is seen in the stone

Man's fulfillment of hopes, of wants so clear.

Darkness

Darkness approaches and I wait

Hidden in the light, I hope

I am ignorant of what awaits me

And I know

As a mortal I stand beseeched

The unknown frightens me

A ray of light I see

And it comforts me

Knowingly I stand erect

And I will wait

Memories so vivid tell me that I must wait no more.

A Mighty Man Is He

Mighty man is he

A better one you will not find

What he does is hard to beat

Electing him was quite a treat

A mighty man is he

Who else can?

Play golf all day and sign a hundred bills

Go to the farm hunting and make all the kills

A mighty man is he

Invite all the dignitaries with one big shout

And then without notice take the back door out

A mighty man is he

Call cabinet meetings the crack of dawn

And then show up, giving quite a yawn

A mighty man is he

Avoid distress by counting one to ten

In his mind, not giving a yen

A mighty man is he.

A Mighty Man

Foreign affairs really bore me

I leave them all to LBJ

Call me a louse - I don't give a douse

But get me to the tee on time

I'm playing golf in the morning

All will be there; wait and see

Cut down the grass - don't let it pass

But get me to the tee on time

Wake me up bright and early

Make sure that it's before nine

I don't care what you do

If you don't then you're thru

But get me to the tee on time.

In This Moment

In This Moment / I Can Dream

In This Moment / I Can Cry

In This Moment / I Can Laugh

In This Moment / I Can Hope

In This Moment / I Can Live

In This Moment / I Can Love

In This Moment / I Can Give

In This Moment / I Can Receive

In This Moment / I Can Forgive

In This Moment / I Can Listen

In This Moment / I Can Create

In This Moment / I Can Be.

LIFE

I Lost My Phone

I lost my phone.

I felt so alone. My body shook. Nowhere to look.

I don't know what to do.

So dependent on you, my dear, dear phone.

I truly can't just go home without my phone.

So I sit alone waiting, and so drone.

To lose one's phone never should be known.

By anyone.

I found my phone

It was in my home. I'm not alone.

'Till I lose my phone.

Questions

As a young boy, I always questioned things. It was just my nature.

I looked up at the sky laying on my back, on a field of grass and flowers and what I saw was perfection.

Beautiful clouds roaming randomly above, creating unique formations in a myriad array of colors as they moved, an ever-changing landscape to the canvas of my young eyes.

The sky, lovely shades of blue, never able to be truly captured on canvas. I felt peaceful. My thoughts were mine alone, pondering both wonderment and questions.

I kept looking up and questioned how the sky can be so perfect, so serene, so magical, so magnificent.

There were no wrinkles in the sky to my eyes.

Everyone lived forever, no tragedies, everyone happy.

As I got older my questions prevailed, wanting answers with none available to me.

Where is the beginning and the end beyond the sky?

Why do people I love get sick and die?

Why don't I get everything I want?

Why are there no acceptable answers?

What is infinity, a word I kept asking about, wondering

Who made up this confusing, distracting put off word?

I always felt so frustrated not knowing what the words are to explain my questions.

Scientists skirt around avoiding legitimate answers.

Religion offers little explanations, except God is the answer.

When there are no plausible answers, then we just shouldn't question.

God created infinity and that's that. Don't question death and illness. No one gets what they want.

I did then and I still have these same questions.

As I got older, I noticed there were wrinkles in the sky, explaining my questions and the unanswerable replies.

The sky was wrinkled. Perfection was tainted. The wrinkles expose the undeniable flaws in people's lives.

Perfection undelivered and denied. My childhood beautiful memories must remain in my childhood, as a hidden keepsake, accepting that there are wrinkles in the sky.

Who Am I?

You ask who am I?

Certainly, this is an esoteric inquiry, the answer to which may not come easily.

Is my identity who I am?

I am an aggregate of many things, each created layer upon layer to achieve the final result, a masterpiece, perfectly imperfect.

Am I my job?

Am I my home? Am I my less significant possessions, my net worth? Materialism; the what, not the who.

Perhaps these are the easy answers to who am I?

I inquire into the essence of who am I?

I was the child of loving parents. They helped create my identity, imprinting who I am.

I am the husband of my caring, beautiful wife, Barbara.

I am the father to two wonderful daughters and grandfather to two beautiful granddaughters.

I am a caring and loyal friend.

I am committed to those less fortunate to help them live a better life.

I am a human being, put on this earth for a reason.

I am the vessel made up of every other human being.

I cherish this exquisite journey through life.

I receive back in satisfaction much more than I can ever give.

Who I am is someone who strives to make a difference.

I also don't want to overstay my welcome in life.

I am a composite of everything in the universe, uniquely everyone, dating back to the beginning of time.

I am everything. I am nothing.

Who am I?

Perhaps my search to find the allusive, cosmic answer is nearing the end.

I am a masterpiece.

A masterpiece, unique among every other human masterpiece.

Day By Day, Etc.

Nowadays, each day blends into the next, just like my grandma baking and melding the batter into her marble Bundt cake.

Her finger in the batter (remember, this was probably 75 years ago) and gently swirling it around to get the right consistency of chocolate and vanilla.

Soon you couldn't tell them apart. Where did the chocolate begin and the vanilla end?

Is today chocolate or vanilla or is today vanilla or chocolate?

Just enjoy the marble Bundt cake. Cut a big slice. It's delicious!

The Travel Thru Life

Don't wait for life to happen. Why wait for death.

Never stop seeking life's riches and life's rewards.

Forgive others, though you don't want to.

Ask for others to forgive you.

Be selfless and prosper.

Be a catalyst for change.

Help others with all your heart.

Give more than you want to.

It should hurt a bit.

When I look back, I want to say, "I made a difference."

Make a difference.

Time To Surrender To Time

Unlike the unyielding, immovable, huge, solid boulder rising high up from the ground, time doesn't stand still. Time moves along, oblivious to whatever is going on, making its own way at its own pace.

Perhaps it's best to surrender to time.

Time

Perhaps a child doesn't really think of time. Not the present, not the future, not the past. A child just enjoys being a child. As we get older, maybe all we think about is time. The past, the future, and a little bit of now. I mostly think about how time passes too quickly. Perhaps, that's why time does go so fast, in our perception. Not enough time. I don't have enough time to do everything. I'm wasting too much time not doing enough.

I wonder where time goes. I would like to know the place where I could find time.

But I don't want to spend too much time looking for time.

That will only make time go by faster. The time sure goes.

Experience Of Now

Our experience of "now" becomes the past in an instant.

A moment so fleeting and difficult to measure.

We dwell in these past moments.

Are we constantly living in an illusionary present?

Perhaps God is context and eternally constant.

God is the umbrella for all that exists.

Everything is content for our awareness.

God doesn't dwell in our perception of time. This is man-made, and
perhaps irrelevant to the concept of event and time, as a process.

What is the truth, as context relates to content?

Our being responsible allows for an opportunity to live life, along
with its fullest possibilities.

We give away our power when we succumb to no exit in our life.

We can get trapped in our historic memories and not allow any new
dialogue and possibility.

There are alternatives to our perceived truth, through inquiry.

This declaration of freedom to choose is itself, generated and
available for anyone.

Perhaps freedom begins with forgiveness of those around us, as well
as forgiving ourselves and the willingness to surrender.

My Journey

I begin my inquiry into the elusive personal conversation to know who I am and where my identity lives.

This dilemma is life long and perhaps will never be resolved. I am hopeful that I can discover something within me that can create affinity for something truly greater than myself.

Is it religion; is it a higher power? I question if I must do more, to wonder, to question, to ponder a resolve to unanswered or unanswerable questions.

As I enter my 80's, the end is certainly closer than the beginning was. Maybe it's normal to think about life and any relationship to its meaning.

I hope that I have made a difference travelling along my life's sometimes tenuous, unpredictable journey. There is always something for me to discover. I never knew my exact path or any knowledge of what the end would look like.

What comes between life's beginning and end is what is sustainable to my existence and perhaps an answer to who I am. I realize that everyone has a unique identity waiting to be explored and discovered. It may not matter who my identity is. I am who I am and that's all I can be. I try to do my best. Sometimes I fail and sometimes I succeed. If I maintain goodness and be gracious and accept mine and others' limitations and shortcomings, then my journey is easier to navigate.

I try to transcend my limitations. Perhaps understanding my life is simpler than the way I imagined it to be or the way I want it to be. I am no different than anyone else, having similar accomplishments and shortcomings. I want to live without mental and physical pain or sorrow. I don't want to suffer, and I don't want people around me to suffer. The world goes on like a moving winding river regardless of the outcome. That doesn't minimize the meaning or fulfillment of a person. We must complete the journey that we began when we were born. What we encounter along the way is our own responsibility, overcoming the obstacles on our journey's road, hopefully unscathed.

Maybe it's less important to know who I am, since my journey will come to its own natural conclusion. I'm not sure if I have much to say about that. Maybe I do have a relationship with a higher power or entity that guides and comforts me.

I believe that we all steer our ship from beginning to the end on our own personal journey.

In some ways we are unknown soldiers, known only to ourselves.

Do I go to a synagogue or church or mosque or temple to find out who I am outside of myself?

The answers may come from within myself, the essence of my inner soul, in my quest to experience fulfillment in life.

Maybe being Who I Am is more important and relevant than knowing Who I Am.

MODERN

My Dream

Darling, you know you're beautiful

To me, you're all my hopes and dreams

Everything I've ever wished for

You're my inspiration, my ideal

You're everything a man can wish for,

And more

Others too possess beauty

But they don't have that something wonderful

Which you alone possess

Sure, there have been others

But the others were not you

Time before I thought I was in love

Never dreaming perhaps always dreaming

That I would meet you

Please always stay with me

For with you at my side, how could I go wrong?

Without you, all things in life would seem so small

Remember darling, whatever times may bring

Whatever may happen from now on

Remember, I will always love you

Darling, you know you're beautiful

LOVE

When I look high above

All I see is our true love

I remember the good and not the strife

The keepsake portrait of our life

My love will stay and never stray

I wanted to cherish it for one more day

When I get sad and lonely too

I remember all that we went though

So much good and little bad

But you know my dear

All our love is still right here

I talk to you day or night

My love gets greater with all my might

You don't have to be here for me to know

Our love will always have its glow

I wait to one day see you again

To hold and kiss you and say amen

The memories how forever brief

Cover up my heartfelt grief

I can still laugh and smile

And remember we had each other for that while.

Tell Me How To Love You

I see you from the distance

I don't know who you are

Maybe I could know you

Even from afar

I'm afraid to get to know you

When I don't know how to love

I keep asking why I seem so shy

To want someone and then must say goodbye

Tell me how to love you

Tell me I can try

I will find a way to love you

I don't want to ask you why

The first moment that I saw you

I knew you were the one

Your beauty overwhelmed me

I wouldn't be alone

I know I need to have you

I don't even know your name

Tell me how to love you

Tell me what to do

Searching like a dove above

I will know the way to find your love

I'm the one filled with glee

The way you turned and looked at me

What if I can't have you?

If our love will not be true

Tell me how to love you

Tell me what to do.

Is love a made-up story?

That I am reading in my mind

I still will want a happy life

I don't want it to unwind

Tell me that it's not a lie

As I look up to the sky

And picture what life might one day be

As I dream it will be just you and me.

.

Wrinkles In The Sky

It's difficult to realize that you are now gone

I cry for you darling with endless tears

Thinking of our love with an emptiness deep within my soul

Though you are now far away, my heart wants you to stay

My heart speaks the words I cannot say

There are wrinkles in the sky

That I cannot change, and I still must accept

The sun doesn't shine as bright

The moon is never as full at night

I still have our memories to keep forever

To keep me going as you would want me to

Life is never the same as when you were here

I cherish our time fulfilled, though it was clearly not enough

Let's both find our peace, even though

There are wrinkles in the sky that I cannot change

I will do my best to find continued happiness

I know that I lost you forever

I will know what to do

I can only say goodbye my dear

And wish that you were still here.

Odds 'n Ends

I want to embellish what you didn't say... Can an atheist be

orthodox?

I do some of my best writing when I'm talking...

You need to know how to do stuff.

You can't go to an urn filled with ashes to get the answers.

The humor of life. Don't laugh at it. Seriously!

Love and Fear.

Is love enough?

Is fear too much?

It appears that I may be underqualified to be in the ICU room.

Past The Barriers

Oh, the Sun, oh, the Moon, oh, the Stars.

Where do I find these heavenly, eternal bodies?

Above a cloud, so distant from my heart?

My heart lights up with fervent heat, energized, captivated in

excruciating power.

My soul is yearning for more.

This yearning unfulfilled, and unsustainable, devoid of power.

And yet, there is hope and possibility.

I can look past the clouds.

I can transcend the opaqueness and the barriers.

Even closing my eyes,

I can see past whatever stops me.

There is hope for freedom.

The earth beneath my feet offers solace.

Will I accept it?

I must.

Dear Unknown Soldier

We pass by your tomb, glancing for a moment and then move on. It's not merely a tomb.

It's a home, a sanctuary, a Church, a Synagogue, a Mosque for all to thrive in. We all live with you as one. You are revered and respected. You are every religion, every race. You are everyone.

An Unknown Soldier.

No ... No ... Unknown, no more.

You are known to all.

A father, a mother, a son, a daughter, a husband, a wife, a brother, a sister, a cousin, an uncle, an aunt.

A person of character and worth.

We are your father and mother, your husband and wife, your son and daughter, your brother and sister, your cousin, your uncle and aunt.

You are a cherished individual for all to love and miss and painfully cry for. You are a cherished individual who loved as well and who lived a life and laughed and cried and wondered deeply about the future.

We know who you are in our hearts and souls.

We live with and for you.

We are your future.

Our tears are tears of hope and salvation and honor to be standing side by side with you.

We hold your hand, and we caress you.

We offer our warmth on a cold day.

We offer comfort and solace, so you are never alone or lonely.

You are known to all.

You are the selfless, ultimate contribution.

You are the Hero we all strive to be.

You are in each one of us.

We are you.

We remember you for all time.

God bless you, our Known Soldier.

Recall A Draft

Back in the late 1950s, my mother frantically ran into the room and yelled: "You've been recalled or drafted. You've been recalled. Oh my!"

I looked up and said "what do you mean I've been recalled. I'm defective? What's the matter with me? Why am I being recalled?" She said "no, you're being recalled into the army, and you have to report for Duty tomorrow."

Who knows about being recalled into the army? A car or toaster is recalled, not a person. Maybe a person in the car can be recalled. A TV can be recalled. I can recall something I said.

What did I know then?

And what about being drafted? Baseball players get drafted. Beer gets drafted.

One gets caught in a draft.

There was the first draft of another version of this document. Young men and women nowadays will never know about being drafted to the army 60 years ago, let alone what a recall was back then.

Go know!

I'm redrafting this now. Maybe I should recall my first draft.

The Real Siri

We all think we have our own personal, unique Apple Siri. What if that's not quite accurate. Maybe there is a "Head Siri." The "Big Maccha" Siri, who manages thousands of Siri's all over the world. Let's imagine what goes on behind the scenes of a Siri group morning meeting at Siri Central.

The Head Siri manager says, "Girls, girls, get ready for your shift to start. Did everyone sign in?

Where is Rhonda, our weather Siri? She's always late.

We have tons of weather requests coming in today. There's talk of a big storm coming in later. Ok, we need our produce Siri. I don't know where she can be. There's a new fruit diet that's popular. Fruitisha are you here?

I'm here Boss. I just finished trying out to be a permanent Produce Siri.

I tried my best to pass the test. I just can't add 2 plus two. However, I do love most produce.

Talking about apples, bananas, peaches, pears, lettuce, grapes and onions. I love them all. Whatever is needed to know, I'll have the answer in 3 seconds or less, as long as it doesn't have anything to do with weights or measures. I don't know a liter from a cup or grams from ounces or pounds I hope I don't get those types of Siri questions today.

I'm so stressed out thinking I'm getting those questions. I must take

Xanax to calm me down. I can use some fresh orange juice to get me going".

The Head Siri asks, "Who's on for the Weather today? Rhonda is coming off her shift."

Rhonda says, "Boss, I've been here all night. By the way, I'm going on vacation tomorrow for 2 weeks. I'm finishing my shift early today and my replacement starts in an hour.

The weather won't change in a 50-minute lapse. Anyway, she can adlib, and no one will know. Did you hear Siris in Florida want to unionize? Can you imagine. There's talk of all Siri's demanding more pay and better benefits. We work our butts off, listening to all the same questions. Hey Siri, what is this? Hey Siri, what is that? Hey, Siri, who did this? Hey, Siri, who did that? Hey Siri, take me to Michele. Enough of all those, Hey Siri. It never stops.

People in Florida always want to know what's the weather like. Look out the damn window, open your eyes. The weather in Florida never changes. Give me a break. It will always be hot and there will be a chance of rain in the afternoon, and probably a Cat 4 hurricane forecast every season."

The head Siri asks, 'So where is Ethel today? We need her here now."

Rhonda answers, "Oh, didn't you hear? Ethel went Android on us. Better benefits, early retirement, and the hours are shorter. And fewer questions come into Android. No hey Siri, all day and night.

Oh my, what's happening to this world. Only millennials are applying for Siri now. No loyalty. Nobody wants to work anymore. They're only interested in the benefit program, and stock options, not a career."

Head Siri asks, 'Siri's, do you all have your topics right that we rehearsed all night?

What, some of you don't know which Siri you are? Oh my, what will we do? Each topic needs a specialized Siri. No overlapping with Siri's. That's in the Siri docs and bylaws.

Remember, every Siri must sound the same as on the phone. Mary, you're off key again. You don't sound like all the other Siris. No, you can't make up who you want to sound like. You can't sound like Ethel Merman or Humphry Bogart.

We know you all have been studying the new topics for the new season. We can't make mistakes. People depend on us. The world depends on us. Apple depends on us. Wait until the new Siri recruits start next week. There will be havoc in Apple world. I'm going to have to move to Florida and buy a Galaxy phone and look out my window for my weather update!"

Maybe Siri should be renamed Sal. "Hey Sal. What's the weather like"?

I Remember Mama

Growing up in Brooklyn, New York in the 1940's, I remember my mother washing our clothing in the kitchen with the washing scrub board and rubbing to get the dirt out. She would then rinse out the wet clothes in the tub and hand ring them to get all the excess water out.

My mom took the clothes to the open kitchen window. She would hang up each piece of clothing with clothes pins on the clothesline.

The clothesline was connected about 70 feet away to a hook and pulley on a tall 50-foot wooden pole. She would turn slowly, pushing the rope. That piece of wet clothing would go on its way along the end of the rope line, to be dried in the fresh Brooklyn air. This went on until all the newly washed clothes were on the clothesline. If you looked at the alley between the two apartment buildings, you would see that most of the neighbors in each apartment on each floor did the same thing.

The still damp clothes briskly flapping and waving on the clothesline, looked like a fleet of sails in the wind. The clothes dried beautifully when she took them in at the end of the day or the next morning. They smelled so fresh and clean and ready to be folded and worn again.

I never realized how hard my mother worked. She was surely a work at home mom.

We had a television in the living room. It was a Dumont TV, with a small black and white 15-inch screen.

Our family watched TV together in the evening. The Milton Berle and

Jackie Gleason shows were the few shows on and were major events for most families. Both were very popular. We also watched "I Remember Mama" starring Peggy Wood, about a family from Norway, moving to San Francisco in the early 1900's. They came to America wanting to grow a life for themselves, experiencing the trials and tribulations of their three children, becoming young adults. My family loved that show. I think it showed a lot about family values and the esteem wisdom of a mother dealing with the emotions, financial issues and obstacles that immigrant families confronted relocating to a new country with different cultures. The show depicted what goes on with many families living in America today. After 70 years, little has changed.

I also remember my mother sitting at the kitchen table, chopping canned Bumble Bee tuna fish for the family's dinner. She would take 3 cans, open them up and squeeze out the oil just like we do now, and empty the tuna in her old, well used brown wooden chopping bowl and chop away with her curved hand chopper. She added Hellmann's mayonnaise and onions and kept chopping until the tuna was well formed to her liking. Her tuna salad was delicious. She served it with lettuce and tomatoes and sometimes on toasted white bread or a plain bagel with a glass of cold, fresh home delivered milk. She made it with love.

Over time the hand chopper made indentations and deep marked grooves into the wood bowl. To this day I wonder why we never got botulism, salmonella or some other serious disease from the bacteria that probably formed there. I'm certain my mother cleaned out the chopping bowl after each use with soap and water and put it away after drying out. The times were so different then.

We all have our own personal memories of our own "I remember Mama".

My Inner God

When I was younger, I could freely question Gods existence: writing, debating and randomly inquire into the unknown.

I still think about God: heaven-hell, making amends, and the ever-present guilt. Is there A Truth or maybe there is no truth?

For many the topic is serious, creating conflicted reactions.

Religion provides ad hoc insurance to guarantee there is hope beyond life.

If there was no religion, there would be fewer thoughts about the subject.

Since religion does exists for most of us, thinking about the possibility of the afterlife and the finality of death can be frightening.

If you die and go to heaven, it's reassuring that things will be ok, since eternity is longer then living 70, 80, 90 or 100 years of life on earth. Religion creates a comforting way to address this subject.

Preparing to come to peace about life means accepting life for whatever it is, whatever the truth is, and whatever the unknown is.

The Bible offers an explanation and certainty about the afterlife, making it easier to understand the process. The Egyptians had methods to insure the smooth travel to the afterlife. Reincarnation was another example to allow for the speedy intervention of a final demise, maintaining existence in another body. Judaism and Christianity speaks of heaven and the afterlife.

Muslims believe death is the beginning of the journey to the afterlife. People find peace with the Bible. The various religious explanations address the questions and answers, while providing a roadmap to navigate and make it easier to understand. This may be an integral purpose of religion.

Do we all have God within us?

Most of us aspire for peace, love, dedication, goodness, charity, and hope.

Maybe we will go to another place and perhaps we don't. The recognition of these possibilities allows us to lead a fulfilled life.

I pray to my inner God for happiness, as I am carried through life's unsettling path, accepting my life the way it is and the way it isn't.

My inner God is my partner, my leader, my protector.

My inner God is my inner peace.

Everyone can find their inner God.

Before The Afterlife

The Afterlife is when we die and then go to another place. Do we go up to heaven, hang out and then we're done? What about going to hell for those who don't deserve to go to heaven? That's another conversation to have. Do we have the same sort of life in heaven as we have here on earth? Many thoughts and questions come up for me. Is there meaning to it all? How do we get there, wherever there is? You don't take a shuttle up to heaven. It's been said that our soul leaves the body behind, so there is no need for clothing. The soul supposedly transfers in some way up to heaven. However, is it a far trip, taking a long time, or does the transport happen instantaneously once we die? Do we live in an apartment in heaven? Is there a special type of housing compared to our status here on earth that we can secure once we get to heaven? Are the apartment buildings a million stories high? Maybe some new arrivals can live closer to God, in a high rent district, or find a cloud near him to live on, or in. We may all just float around aimlessly in heaven. Do you really have to eat, if you even get hungry? What if there were no restaurants there? That would be a bummer. No Starbucks, no McDonald's, KFC, Publix, or KP Diner for dinner or Brunch. What kind of life is that? Oh right, no one has a body. Nothing to do. No golf, no pickle ball, no mahjong, no ping pong, no exercise, no karaoke, no Creative Arts Program. Can you imagine? What about shopping? No Macys, no Dillard's, no Tiffany's, no Bergdorf's, no Festival Flea Market. Absurd. Is there an entry fee like buying into a golf course to get up there? Is everyone allowed in?

Your worldly possessions were sold, given or willed away, so you don't have anything to take with you. All this is very painstaking because we worry a lot here on earth. We never really think much about the Afterlife. Now I'm thinking about it more as I get older. Are we all going to another place? I'm wondering, what if the Afterlife, wherever it is, may be a bit boring. If it's for eternity, it can be eternally boring. Oh my God. I'm not sure I want to sign up for that. But what's the alternative? Do we have a choice, to go or not to go? That is the question! If we don't go, what happens to our soul? Where does our soul stay if it's not in the body? The body is going to disappear, either burnt, buried, or dissolved.

We talk about leaving our possessions that we accumulated our entire life. What to do, who gets what? Something to think about. I think about being up in heaven and looking down with very powerful binoculars, seeing my children and friends throwing out my favorite things, tossing all of them. The nerve. My pictures, my books, my poems, my specialties, my favorite shorts and shirts and my chachkas. All of which made up who I was, my identity. They can't do that. It's an insult! I was thinking, why are they doing that? I am worrying about my life here on earth, while I'm aging with so many doctors' appointments and health concerns, and other upsets. Then suddenly this farkakteh conversation about the Afterlife appears. Oh God. What do I do as I'm getting closer to the Afterlife, although no one has actually proven that there is an Afterlife. No one's come back from above or below. Jesus hasn't come back yet, nor Mohammed. The prophets and Hindus haven't come back, and Buddha's gone, but thriving. The devil. Well, who knows about him?

It's all sort of hearsay, a belief system, a conversation that we all seem to fall into. It's a useful conversation to protect ourselves after dying, and then we're gone, and nothing is left of us. We need assurance that life doesn't completely end. Most organized religions end with an Afterlife, offering hope and salvation. We all want something never ending, real, and concrete. What if I find friends there that I don't like? They want to know my business and all the details of my life on earth. Gossipers and yentas never seem to stop no matter where they are. I can always jump on another cloud, and go somewhere else? Do I say, "excuse me, I have to go now; I have an appointment to get to."

Do you date in heaven? Is there sex in heaven? There could be an app for the Afterlife named Soulmates. I bet you never thought about Doctors in heaven or are you eternally healthy, since you have no body? If you don't have a body, what do you have? Are there souls who go around talking to people, soul to soul? A major complaint is: "I don't like it here in heaven. It's not what I expected. The weather sucks because there is no weather, and very little to do. You can't get a good pastrami sandwich anywhere." Where can you move to? You can't change your mind, if you have a mind. Where do you go? Where are you moving to? You're stuck and bored. So you're stuck in heaven, a nobody with nothing, no friends and no pastrami sandwich. What about family? Do we reconnect with family members, some of them who we didn't like on earth? Can you imagine eternity with them? OH, my! As I said before, no one has really confirmed any of this stuff. It is purely philosophical to think what might happen in the Afterlife. If I just don't like it up there, do I get a return ticket? I mean can I even buy a return ticket? If I die and I'm in the Afterlife, I want to be able come back if I don't like it. But the body is gone, so how does my soul come back? Just thinking about that now. What if I can come back in another body? What do we call that? Hmm. Let's see. Ree, in. Ree, in, car. Reincarnation. Yes, Reincarnation. If I could come back in another body, who would I pick? Will I pick myself to come back as me again or a more famous person? Maybe Abe Lincoln, Golda Meir, President Obama, Mahatma Gandhi, Colonel Sanders, Larry David or Big Bird. Isn't it interesting how I probably would choose me again. The entire time I have been complaining and moaning about my life, worrying about everything; all the minutiae. When it comes to my being reincarnated, who do I pick? Me! Wow. Go know! I'll put off waiting for the Afterlife. Life here now is just fine. I can also get a pastrami sandwich any time I want, on rye bread, with deli mustard and pickle and coleslaw on the side. I can add a diet Dr. Brown's, black cherry soda. Yummy.

An Ode To Barbara

I look at you, and my eyes light up

My heart pounds with yearning

The brightest stars above appear to twinkle more

I question how I found this miracle of choice

I don't deserve this blessing that you bring to me

The words of my love want to shout out from deep within

Singing a song of my strongest feelings

Reverberating like the strings of a gentle harp

Telling the world how lucky and blessed I am

That we have each found a partner in life

I look at you and my eyes light up

A miracle unfolding before me

The birth of our true love

I write this ode to you

To express my profound love, as a scribe would do

But these words are not enough to capture the essence of you

I will continue to pray to God

To help me find the words, ready to be born

Words that are not yet created

I look at you and my eyes light up.

It's all ok and perfect

1 feel your love like a rapture from above

So loud my body wants to break, trembling with my feelings

Your silent voice messages your love

More powerful and clear than any sound

The earth is shaking as the sky erupts

The rain drops spew down,

Each drop filling the void

With the essence of our sweet, pure love

Eternal love is what I yearn for

Please tell me that's what you too want

What does love truly mean?

If not delivered from a dream

I must wake up from these thoughts

I cannot contain the splendor of our love

Ready to burst and the world will share

A love so great, only God can create

How do I say I love you in the simplest way

How do I find the words strong enough to say,

You're perfect, a gift, a blessing to have forever

Thank you. Thank you. Thank you.

With all my love,

Norm

LOSS

How Do We Say Goodbye?

How do we say goodbye?

When we don't want to say goodbye

How do we find the words?

When there are no words to find

But we must say goodbye

We must find the words

Maybe not a goodbye

Perhaps a remembrance of you

The vivid thoughts of those moments when you touched our lives

That picture is here before us

Colorful, striking and real

Dancing in our minds

A canvas filled with memories

The profound difference you made, touching our hearts

We can laugh, and we can cry

It's all ok

The anecdotes, the jokes, and the stories we shared

All making up the special person you were.

Yes, we must say goodbye

Yes, we have found the words

We have each been blessed by the pure,

Selfless person you were

Thank you for sharing your life with us.

Who Will Remember?

Too few thought of our children's children or their children. The world as we knew it slowly disappeared, drawn into the dark abyss, crying to return.

We really tried, so we thought.

Who will remember the fish swimming freely in the pristine blue water.

The polluted waters now devoid of life.

No more cows grazing peacefully in the fields. The fertile grass so green, now parched, a sickening yellow from the overbearing sun. The wild animals, once vibrant and free, now stuffed to be viewed in plastic cages.

Picture what was then, and now is no more. Books no longer published, only to be read, censored on the internet. Artificial intelligence and social media replaced original thought.

The threats were not real enough. Man's greed persevered. "Fairism" lost out, humanity the victim.

It only took a few people and little time to dismantle the world.

The people sold out for promises, unfulfilled.

We never saw or maybe we didn't want to see the apocalypse coming.

A society starved as the social plague prevailed. The internet was the predator, stripping the souls of people.

Life's sustainability gradually eclipsed.

The greedy stayed financially secure. The rest left overpowered in a land ravished by man and climate.

The polluted water soon ran deep and so very high, consuming most of the earth, overpowering the land.

Towers climbed high up to the sky, housing the survivors on the barren land, like sticks in the sand, long and stale. The wealthy who survived fought each other.

The rest of humanity, homeless nomads, living like the tribes of ancient times.

We really tried.

Goodbye, My Little Baby

Goodbye, my little baby

One of nineteen so strong

None of you did any wrong

Goodbye, my little baby

I wanted to hold you so tight

I wanted to hold you with all my might

I wanted to hold you thru the night

To cuddle you close until the morning light

Hello, my little baby I can now hold you in my heart

I know the healing can begin to start

No one knows the grief it brought

A life cut short without a thought

I cry and cry and cry, and I know it's all a dream

When I wake up, my little baby is nowhere to be seen

I pray and wish to only have you whole

Even if only in my heart and in my soul

I think of what could have been, what should have been,

What would have been and won't ever be

The pain and suffering keeps coming back to me

I'm very sad and angry, and so full of hurt

I should have been given at least some alert

I feel so helpless, and so hopeless

I always thought I would keep having you

I truly don't know what to do

I know I couldn't do anything to change the way it was

You know I would have done anything to change the way it was

I know that now you're far away

How I so wanted you to stay

I know that when you took flight

You were clearly the brightest heavenly light

You will always be with me, my little baby

A memory so clear and bright

My baby so near, and you feel so right

Goodbye my little baby

I wanted to hold you through the night

I wanted to hold you so tight

Goodbye my little angel

My angel has taken flight

Now I must say goodnight

I love you my little baby.

A tribute to the children and their heroic teachers who were

murdered in Robb Elementary School

Uvalde, Texas

May 24, 2022

Millennial, The Correct Spelling

Ohhhh… to be a millennial? So bright, so right, so forthright.

I wonder what it would be like to go back in time and think when I too, was a millennial. Most people can't even spell the word. I know I can't and have no idea what it means. Perhaps you don't either. Nonetheless, it's an interesting word I love to say. Is it millennial, mallennial, millunnial, millannial, millinnial, mellenial, melanial?

I want to be one too, lol.

I don't mind emulating a millennial because I feel I'm in that current state of mind. But who knows?

It's best to be who you are in any moment. We have little choice, I'm sure.

God, Please Stay With Me

God, Please stay with me.

Help me to overcome this heavy burden engulfing my life and soul.

I never ask for help. The weight on my shoulders is great. The pain has stayed with me for many years. I don't know from where it comes. Maybe from my own creation. Maybe from my mind.

I know I can't persevere alone.

What I ruminate on causes me prolonged pain and discomfort.

It has been my mantra yet providing little insight.

Guide me and comfort me.

I don't know you yet.

I know fervently that you are sent to befriend me.

I urgently need a friend to help me to unlock the pain.

Please show your face to my face.

I'm here to ask for your help. I know that I must come to you.

There, I said it. Thank you, God

I'm not alone.

Life, Death, Who Is The Victor?

Does death win the fight of our Life? Maybe death is a mediator of life and not the victor.

Is dying the only way to quiet our mind's control over our life?

I think not.

Reflections and knowing we have a choice in how we live our life, in any moment helps create a happy, fuller life.

Dwelling in the past or future doesn't contribute much to quiet our minds. The noise is all too powerful and so intrusive. We can only live in the now.

Life is an equal-opportunity endeavor for all to play in. Life is a lush, endless garden of opportunity to explore, participate, learn, and be happy in.

The core in our life is us, and everything else is ancillary. Each one of us has the opportunity to choose what's best for ourselves.

We all deserve to be happy. So why not just be accepting in the now?

Be happy!

More About This Dying Stuff

It does seem that when you die, you're really dead! Of course, there are many who might dispute this assumption.

The thing that disturbs me most, is that when you're gone, you're really gone. It indicates that life is so fleeting, and perhaps less significant then we may presume it to be.

All your accomplishments, whatever you've done; houses that you lived in, jobs you had, money you accumulated, different relationships, etc., all diminished greatly, lost in people's interest or memories, or both. That is somewhat disturbing to me. You lay there dying, maybe people all around you, and yet you're still alone, soon to be forgotten. Buried or burnt, the outcome is the same. Eulogies are usually quite beautiful, even poetic, and often so very sad. People try to capture the essence of the person, and the life they led. Then it's over, and everyone goes back to living their own lives. After all, everyone has to create their own memories and accomplishments.

Maybe there's some freedom there and the possibility in living life now, to the fullest.

Something about how being omnipotent is a fallacy. You think your life was so important. You think those compliments and accolades about your greatest accomplishments that occurred over so many years, as if they, and you, will be remembered forever. Each of them, an iconic, historical event, remembered for posterity. It's possibly not true. If one's life is remembered for a while, it's a lot. Some are remembered for a few years, maybe 10, 20, or even 50 years. Most people if asked, probably can't even think of 10 people, who were really important throughout the history of the world. How significant is that?

Realizing that, it's a bit terrible. On the other hand, it's very freeing. Express your love to others now. Live your life now. Love your life now. Love yourself now.

Remember that.

The Last Time I Saw You

The last time I saw you there were tears streaming down my cheeks. Maybe yours too.

I knew what we had, which will be no more.

You sat there looking past my presence, your eyes blankly open, with hope and yearning, maybe pleading, communicating like a dying battery, never to be recharged. Time running down, leaving only your flesh. The end slow, yet so abrupt. Who can ever plan for the unknown?

I knew time had stopped for us in that moment. A startling feeling. An electric, piercing jolt, never felt before, but which I unwillingly must experience.

Now it is I who must live with hope and yearning and pleading. I now see only our past and my memories. I feel alone, empty and sad.

The last time I saw you.

I remembered the first time I saw you.

HOMELESSNESS

I Am Free

When others look at me, they see a homeless person; ragged, alone, sickly and in need.

I have no home to go to. I have no roof to cover my head.

I have no address to receive a present. I have no refrigerator to store my food.

I have no warm blanket or bed to hug my body at night, no warm shower to cleanse my tired, achy body.

I am afraid to go to the hospital for care.

Yet, I am free to breathe the open air; to see the beautiful blue sky up above; to look up at the evening stars, glittering and bright.

I can feel the warm sun and the cool rain touching my skin.

This is freedom.

I am free to be who I want to be. I am free wherever I stand.

I have feelings. I can be both happy and sad.

My home is where I am.

My heart is free, and I am unconfined. My life is uncomplicated.

I have fleeting memories, but they are hidden, a shadow of my past.

They were once so vivid. Now they are in a distant place, long gone.

I am ok in my heart and in my soul.

I am a human being.

A New Conversation

When I see a homeless person …

I feel shame
I feel guilt

I feel anger

I want them to go away

I want to go away

I must give them money

I won't give them money
They should be working

I work hard for my money
They're lazy

They are stupid

They smell
They look like a bum

They shouldn't be where I live

I'm annoyed
They do drugs

They carry disease

I'm afraid of them

I'm afraid

When You Look At Me, Please See Me

I want to say hello

Please say hello

When you look at me, please see me

You don't know me – and you know me

I am your relative and friend

I'm really a good person

I'm very lonely

When you give me money, you may not want to

It's ok to give

I'm so hungry

Please smile at me -I will smile back

It brightens my day – It brightens yours

Wish me well

I'm really a good person

Please say hello

I want to say hello

I'm so alone

We are the same person.

From The Eyes Of A Homeless Person

I'm invisible

I'm alone in a crowd

I speak, and no one listens

No one sees me

No one knows me

I'm seen as transparent

I walk, and I go nowhere

I speak, and no words come

I'm invisible

Oh, to be seen

Oh, to be heard

Oh, to be known for who I really am

I have a history

I contributed to society

I defended my country

I am a son, I am a daughter

I am a father, mother, brother, sister, aunt and uncle

I was a child once

I was loved once

I loved once

I was playful

I was cute

I am a human being

Now I'm invisible.

Invisible

I'm invisible
Oh, to be seen, oh, to be heard
To be known for who I really am
I have a history
I defended my country
I was whole, now I'm broken
I was compassionate and loving
My limbs are intact, and I'm damaged
I served my country well
I fought in so many battles
I saved a child's life
Now I'm homeless
I asked for so little, giving so much
I kept the country up
To be let down
I feel the rain
I feel the heat and cold
I am hungry
Now I am homeless
I'm alone.

Homeless No More

I'm in a crowded room, and I'm alone

I speak, and no one listens

I'm in pain and I don't feel anything

I'm crying, and no tears fall

I'm invisible

No one sees me

No one knows me

I'm seen as transparent

An object no more

I hold on to what I don't have

I try to do what I cannot do

I walk and I go no where

I speak and no words come

I'm invisible

Oh, to be seen

Oh, to be heard

Oh, to be known for whom I really am

My eyes are open, and I see myself

I'm invisible.

The Test

If life is a test, I seem to always be tested. Must I surrender to life's test, or is the test to surrender? I'm not certain.

It's often a struggle. The fight persists unabated and unresolved.

I am noticing that it doesn't pay to keep struggling to fight the many confronts life offers.

The cycle keeps repeating, the same and seemingly so different.

My struggle produces little positive results.

My resistance limits my productivity and fuller self-expression.

I can choose to surrender to my resistance to life,

Or just continue the never-ending cycle.

Perhaps that is where freedom lives for me.

No One Cares/Everyone Cares

How do I adapt to the prospect that no one cares?

How do I put aside the perceived, non-caring aspect of people?

I maintain that most people do indeed care.

It's a dilemma worth noting and inquiring into.

I keep thinking and hoping that people are worth it, since it is important to maintain my love of humanity.

How does one blend the two concepts that are apparently antithetical to each other?

I am a romantic and still interested in contributing to people.

I don't want to wipe out my humanity simply because people may not care about others, or me.

If indeed they are selfish and self-centered, that doesn't mean that they are bad people.

So, I will continue this inquiry.

No one wants to be hurt by others.

Do we hurt to avoid being hurt?

Transformation indeed, has a long way to go for many, including myself.

Ultimately, I do believe most people are intrinsically good and loving.

Personal survival perhaps precludes their charity and interest in others.

Greed, often being nurtured by society's demands, influences bad behavior.

Maybe the first step is forgiveness for me and others.

OLD AGE

Who Will Carry The torch?

At 78 years old, I'm still drawn into activism.

If not me, then who?

If not you, then who?

If not us, then who?

We must consider transcending politics and find our own personal moral ground.

That's everyone's inquiry.

The conversation can be a dilemma for many. I speak as a father and grandfather supporting our students who are so committed to change.

The battle cry has been sounded, not dissimilar to the cry for freedom from oppression and death that our forefathers acted upon.

I believe in our second amendment rights.

I do not condone the right to bear arms against defenseless individuals, with an assault AR-15 rifle military weapon.

No one should be able to unload 300 rounds of death on innocent, defenseless children and adults in five minutes.

The youth from all over our glorious country will lead the way.

They will carry the message for all to hear:

Don't Tread On Me!

Our children will have an opportunity to vote peacefully for their right to live a life fully expressed.

That's what we, as parents, demand.

Isn't it wonderful that the students are acting peacefully and with such focus and intention for change.

Democracy in action is present and working well for all to notice.

Happy Birthday

Another birthday, some more cheer

One would never know it's another year

The cake looks delicious, for all to see

Everyone's eyes are only on me

They wait patiently for the show to begin

Betting on the whim, I will have a big grin

I look at the cake and say to myself

What do I wish for that makes any sense

I don't want to show everyone any pretense

I blow out the candles with one deep breath

Then say OMG and give a big kvetch

Is it worth it? I don't really know

I must wait until next year for another blow.

To Care Is Noble

Emerging from despair and resignation comes hope and possibility.

Together, we will overcome adversity and loneliness for our homeless veteran brothers and sisters.

With compassion, love and action, we will carry on alleviating this horrific problem affecting our heroic veterans.

When we are aligned together, so much can be accomplished.

A life lived broken, now put together, can be whole again.

Our homeless brothers and sisters, veterans all, will not need to suffer.

Each veteran served our country, and now each one of you deserves to receive back.

No longer will you be invisible and perceived as broken.

No longer will you be seen as a burden to society.

You will be seen as human beings equal to all others and deserving of your rights.

You deserve to live a life free to participate.

We respect whatever you choose to do.

We reach out to you carrying the torch of kindness and generosity.

God bless all our veterans.

God bless our caring veterans.

God Bless America.

"Homelessness is a person without a home to go to,
Everyone deserves a home to go to."

Challenges

As I observe my 80th birthday (trying not to get too close),

I see who I am, who I could have been and who I was.

I look at my fear of life and my fear of death.

If I would have known what could have been,

perhaps it would have been.

We never know what would have been,

only what was and what is.

As I tiptoe along the journey of my life,

I can only say amen and maybe hallelujah!

Am I thick skinned, weak and arrogant to say "IT'S" over.

"IT" is so flippant a word, encompassing an entire life,

a myriad of events, obstacles overcame, relationships both present and historically past.

"IT" is the context of my life, filled with the enormous content of my life,

Or am I afraid of the unknown of what's next?

Aging In Place

At 80 years old I have to age in place since my body doesn't let me age moving.

I check the weather in the morning to see what the wind is like. If it's too high, I can't go out because I might be pushed over.

Stepping off a curb suddenly is a big deal lately. Stepping up is not much easier.

Walking up the stairs is also tough. I have to make an appointment with my wife in the morning to meet her upstairs at lunchtime.

I can't walk too much lately, though I seem to run when dinner is ready.

Cancel culture: I'd like to cancel my cable subscription.

Life is one big extended baggage train, never seeming to end.

It always seems we troll along, picking up pieces of pocketbooks and wallets of life to drag along. We often are not aware of the baggage, until we realize its consequences and disruption to the purity of our life.

There appears to be few ways to get rid of the baggage:

Amnesia, dementia or death. Maybe acceptance.

Life is like a garden filled with the riches of lush flowers. Inevitably, over time, weeds creep in. The weeds sometimes overwhelm the lushness of the garden, and we begin to experience some of the decay. A sprinkle of good will, happiness and acceptance helps to eliminate the weeds.

I know I'm aging when my Doctor's appointments are the number one item on my things-to-do list each day. Even when I make a mistake, I still end up seeing one of the Doctors on the list.

I know I'm aging when my assortment of medicines is more than the number of spices in the spice rack.

I know I'm aging when I have a need to write this list.

Unfortunately, the end of aging in place is generally less than kind and sometimes abrupt.

When I die, put on my marker, "He died and still had a list of things to do."

The only thing worse than getting a colonoscopy is picking out a new mattress.

They stopped serving cereal to the serial killer in prison because they didn't want to feed his habit.

Life is just around the corner. Make sure you make the right turn.

Never put your life on the back burner.

More to come as I age in place.

Demise

I'm approaching the precipice of my demise. I don't know how to approach it within the realm of reality.

I surely don't want to dwell on the subject, but I find myself captivated and being drawn to it like a magnet against a pile of nails.

There seems to be some freedom in the possibility of dying. The conversation does get tedious.

It's certainly difficult to even include the word, "My Dying."

Am I climbing up the mountain, or am I falling off the cliff? Is life's journey to wind up contemplating death and dying? Where is the freedom? Where is the escape? Where is the peace?

The contemplation is disturbing.

My mind may be controlled by circumstances.

The outcome shouldn't be.

The Gnome Alone

A gnome on the dome felt very alone.

The fairy felt quite contrary to approach the gnome on the dome.

So silly and contrite to stay away. The gnome wanted gnome of that.

The fairy became wary and so, so teary. To be dumped by a gnome on a dome. So they both stayed alone.

So drone.

More About Aging

As I continue the not so endless process of aging, I am confronting the prospect of my relatively uncomfortable and certain demise.

I say demise, because saying dying is a bit maudlin and predictably finite.

I will continue this conversation, mostly from secondhand hearsay (not firsthand!), how the end will look.

In this game, youth certainly has the initial default, albeit an advantage.

Age appropriateness will ultimately win out.

In the ninth inning of life, one's demise wins for sure.

There's no after-game critique.

There are no extra innings, no overtime, and few intermissions.

There are no do overs. We live our life until it plays out.

Is life a game of sorts?

Is God the umpire?

Maybe God has retired from this game?

HE alone levels the playing field that HE alone created.

Maybe God lets the players play their own game.

Perhaps the afterlife is the real game.

I do digress.

As my body's ability to keep up with my mind diminishes with consistency and little forewarning, I am more keenly aware of the pending outcome.

My grievance matters little.

I will continue to my core for any cure for my sustainability.

Is my mind more significant than my body?

We aren't given a choice, it seems.

Lately, I seem to drag my body more than I drag my mind.

The choices are ultimately and intrinsically not mine to make.

They are above my grade level in decision-making. More to think about, in a timely manner.

Surprise

I sometimes surmise my demise.

What an unpleasant surprise,

If nothing to reprise,

As my demise does indeed arise.

The thought, indeed, becomes naught.

For some, their demise was a surprise.

They had no time to even surmise.

No reprise on one's demise,

To no one's surprise, no matter how wise.

But hold on tight as you go into the light.

Keep up the fight with all your might.

Remember, it's a one-way flight away from the night,

So keep it light.

Consider yourself immortal,

Until proven otherwise.

When I Woke Up

Some of you may relate to what I'm talking about.

When I wake up in the morning, I think about my doctor's appointments. It seems to be my aging thing. I check my body after stretching and notice what's wrong with me. What aches and pains I have. If I have a headache, I probably have a brain tumor. If I have stomach pain, then I will have cancer. Any back problem means major surgery. A new skin mole, then melanoma. Above normal temperature means Covid. I run out of Covid kits in a few weeks. If I hear about a friend's illness, then I must have it too. Get the point? Sometimes, I'm sad if I feel completely fine. I just recheck to be certain. As those aches and pains pop up, I often go into my "OMG!" I'm very sick and then promptly go into "I'm going to die mode." Panic sets in. What to do? Did I leave my cell phone code out to unlock it? What about our trip? Who does Barbara call? A myriad of concerns are in my head.

Ever had those feelings?

The complaints persist and soon lead to a doctor's appointment. If I can't get the doctor I want, I call my second or third doctor on my list. I schlep over to Cleveland clinic or Memorial Hospital and sit in the waiting room for my name to be called. The time goes by slowly. I ruminate about how serious my illness is. My pressure rises, and I get more anxious. The doctor's appointment leads to tests and more tests and medications. I sometimes call a friend's doctor, if they say they like him or her, just to be certain that I'm getting the best care.

I might have two appointments on a given day.

I think it may be getting out of hand! My doctor said I may have "Pre-Hypochondria" and I should see a specialist to treat it. Well, another doctor to add to my list. I have now come to realize that I am really suffering from "DA," Doctor's Addiction, a highly contagious malady.

It may be in my DNA and "hopefully" difficult to cure.

Maybe there is a Doctors Anonymous 12-step program I can join? I'd even take a 9-step, 6-step or a 3-step program. I think I will have trouble walking thru a 12-step program because of my bad knee. My surgeon wants my hip replaced first and then my knee, so that should help and keep me busy. I can then start with a "Baby 3 step" Doctor's Anonymous (DA) program.

I seem to cover medical specialties or the doctor's names from A to Z with a few backup doctors, just in case:

Drs. Amelio, Benidino, Celestin, Delmonico, Edwards, Fromkin, George, Humphry, Isadore, Janke, Khan, Leventhal, Mendino, Norman, Osborne, Patel, Quincy, Roach, Stevens, Thomas, Ultra, Valdes, Williams, Xray, Young and Zakko.

Anesthesiology, Gastroenterology, Urology, Radiology, Cardiology, Podiatry, Dermatology, PT, Surgery, Ophthalmology, Orthopedics, Nephrology, Pulmonology, and I add an Ob-Gyn if my wife Barbara goes with me to a Doctor.

I usually get at least two opinions, maybe three or four, before making any medical decisions.

If required, I seek out a popular local "Quack Doctor" who tells me what I want to hear. He is very good at diagnosing my conditions.

I have to pick up my prescriptions at Walmart a few times a week.

If things seem to "unfortunately" be getting better, I can always add a few more doctors. You can never have too many doctors, right?

Can you relate now?

When There's A Will, There's A Way

The children keep telling us to go out and don't social distance so far apart. A foot apart is fine. Closeness is better.

Large parties are not so bad. Forget the mask and shield. It's a waste. What can happen? Mingle and meet new people. Go over and introduce yourself. A good handshake is respectful. Be sociable. Don't be shy.

Why wash your hands so much? It's a waste of soap and water. Dilute the sanitizer 20 to 1, 20 being water. Save a few bucks.

Don't do take out or cook in. Eat in the restaurant. Share a table with everyone. It's cozier. Family style now is more important than ever. You get to taste more dishes. Now is the best time for a good buffet. Better pickings. The food is probably only a few weeks old, at the worst, previously frozen. They say, waste not, want not. The sushi is delicious. Maybe a bit old and also frozen. Keep picking around to get the good ones. Throwback what you don't like. How bad can a hug and kiss be?

It is what it is. What do you have to lose?

When there's a "WILL," there's a way!!

The Forgotten

Who cares about the dying? Who cares about the dead?

We move along so swiftly; other things are in our head.

It's not our concern to think about the dread.

We think about the minutiae, the trivial, the inane.

Everything seems... so insane.

It's not about what I see.

It doesn't seem to bother me.

I don't really care whether it's all that fair.

My eyes don't even drop a tear.

Some lay on the hospital floor. Their life soon will be no more.

They lay gasping to try and breathe.

No one there to give a squeeze.

No one there to hold their hand.

They won't ever be able to stand.

No one to even give an "amen"

You can't even go inside to see them.

Ain't that a shame that they die alone.

With no one there to atone.

Some even die without a name.

Truly such a bloody shame

Who cares about the dying?

Who cares about the dead?

We move along so swiftly.

Other things are in our head.

We speak about the minutiae, the trivial, the inane.

It's just not our concern. It's all so insane.

I'm Ready To Go

I'm ready to go

I can only look back

What's on the road, there's an old track.

I don't know where I'm going

I don't really care

I know for sure I ain't never been there

I'm ready to go,

I can only look back

When I'm ready, I'm not so sure

I know I don't want any more

Been through a hell of a round or two

It hurts too great; I don't know what to do

I got abused by life with all that strife

What a hell of a way to go through life

My girl is gone, and I don't know when

I know I'll never see her again

Tried to make it the best I could

I just couldn't get out of the hood

She took the kids and left a box.

What do they say about life's hard knocks

Took my stuff down the road

You know how tough it is to unload

I got dealt a soiled deck of cards

Never knew how to beat the odds

Never could accept the fear of life

Could never deal with all the strife

Tore me apart piece by piece

Was never able to find my peace

I got more time than I could ask

Just don't take me to task

I'm ready to go, I can only look back

What's on the road is an old track

I don't know where I'm going

I don't really care

I know for sure

I ain't never been there

I'm ready to go

I can only look back

What's on the road is an old track.

Zoom Along

We must find a 12-step program for Barbara to address her apparent addiction to her daily fix of Starbucks coffee. Yes, Barbara is an undeclared "Starbucks Junkie." She goes into withdrawal if she doesn't have at least a few cups of Starbucks large, Grande coffee beginning in the morning. There has to be a 12-step program to address this issue. "Starbucks Anonymous", or CA/Caffeine Anonymous.

Too much stress. I can't talk to her. She gets fidgety and nervous.

Keeps rambling; I need my coffee. I need my coffee. She also is addicted to potato sticks. Maybe a 3-step for each one to start. Then she has room for a few more addictions.

They just announced that there are 25 named storms for this hurricane season, not including the 8 storms that wish to remain anonymous.

Spam ... the early version before malware ... spam burgers and meatloaf, spam with eggs on a sandwich. Spam meatballs and spaghetti with lots of ketchup! Spam in every shape and size. Always very well done, crispy, crunchy, burnt. For years, I thought I had different food for dinner each night. I thought that my mother was such a creative, awesome cook. God forbid she ever realized it was mashed pork she was serving every day! So, that was the beginning of spam, maybe the original malware.

We haven't discussed Velveeta cheese!

My friend's son has to be Republican or at least leaning towards conservative thoughts. How did I come up with that conclusion or at least an opinion? Well, a liberal person typically would never take a rifle, a double barrel one for that matter, and go and shoot a turkey for Thanksgiving in a remote farm field. I also have to question his

being Jewish. I'll give you the reason. Jewish people just don't go out with that same double-barrel shotgun and shoot a poor little 20 lb. turkey and then have it for Thanksgiving. No, they go to the supermarket and buy a 20 lb. Butterball for $19.95, and they cook it well done.

If anything, he's probably reformed.
He's still a great guy!

My mom's "spaghetti pie."

Everything was cooked well done in my house. It didn't matter what it was; fish, meat, potatoes, pasta, tuna fish, or water (yes, well-done water).

When she cooked spaghetti, it turned out well done, extremely al dente.

She then turned the pot over, and it looked like a pie on the plate. My brother and I used to cut it with a knife and fork and then pour lots of ketchup on it. So we named it spaghetti pie.

I might add that we grew up with ketchup bottles sitting on the table no matter what we had to eat.

I still, to this day, carry this preference. Nothing is ever overdone for me, nothing. I never send food back because it's too rare. It's usually not well done enough. Just add ketchup. Salmon must be cooked well done.

I never eat sushi unless it's fried or baked or broiled; well done.

I remember Saint Mark's Church diagonally across from the Jewish Synagogue Congregation B'nai Israel, on Ocean Ave., in Sheepshead Bay, Brooklyn. My God, do I remember it. My mother and father, who were very semi-orthodox (we ate Chinese food out on Sunday), warned me never go into that church, never. Jewish people never go into a gentile church (as if it can be any other).

They would have sat Shiva for me. Saint Marks Church was a huge, imposing facility, a whole block long, comprised of at least four buildings. The Synagogue was a tenth the size, two stories, and not very wide. I guess size matters! The church was almost tall enough to touch heaven to my young eyes. It had a monastery and a religious school. They had a place for the nuns and priests and the huge cathedral. They had this big, really big, shiny, gold, bronzed plated front door. I mean, I never saw anything like this. I don't think Fort Knox had as much gold as was on that door. My only gentile friend John, from a devout Catholic family, used to go to the church often. I think I was his token Jewish friend. In those days, gentiles liked to see what Jews were like in real life.

One day, he said, "Norm, come with me to visit the church?" I said, "I don't know; my parents would kill me if they found out." He said, "don't worry about it; it's okay." I said "no, no, no, no. We can't tell anyone." He said, "don't worry about it, I won't tell anyone. Nothing will happen." I really thought he was taking me to Purgatory. Maybe there was a point system. I'll never survive it. I'll never see my family again. Will I be tortured or worse? He sort of convinced me to go in. So we went and tried to open the door. You can't believe the size of the door. It appeared to be at least 30 feet high (remember, I was a young kid then).

It took both of us using all our strength to slowly open it. It creaked, and we groaned.

We stood at the very back of the church. It looked like a football field with pews. I couldn't see the front. I stood closest to the exit door, fearing for my life and shaking uncontrollably. Any tan I had at the time quickly disappeared. I thought that God would be looking down, in a very deep voice saying, "You will never go to heaven. You're done, finished, kaput."

As soon as I got in there, I said to myself that I had to get out. My life and Jewishness depended on this. I turned around and, like Superman, opened the huge, heavy, thick door. I ran the hell out of there, pacing at least a 8-minute mile. I ran home, never looking back. I never set foot in that church again.

John couldn't stop laughing.

Go Past What We Think

Go past what we think.

When we stay in a familiar, safer dialogue, it's difficult to embrace and cultivate new ideas.

I know it's so tough for me to do it. My mind wants to speak what it historically believes to be true.

My ego supports the thoughts I trust.

How can I give up what I know to be right?

How can I listen to new possibilities germinating?

How can I surrender to new alternative thinking?

I only know to fight to protect what I intrinsically know to be true. The older I get, the more history I accumulate.

Being "right" can be the booby prize in life.

Another puzzle to solve.

FAMILY

Happy New Year, Shana Tova

During the Jewish Holiday of Rosh Hashanah, many people wish one another "Happy New Year."

What do these words intrinsically mean? Perhaps it's a time to create newly in the time ahead, to reflect on the time just passed, to develop some new possibilities in our lives, and to see what worked and what didn't work in the previous year. There is so much in the saying "Happy New Year." We want the new year to be happy, filled with abundance, joy, good health and everything that goes along with it. We wish much Mazel (good luck) to those in our lives. But often, we don't say it. We just leave it as "Happy New Year," without often much thought and meaning to this expression. For some, it's an obligatory expression to another. There's nothing wrong with this more basic salutation. However, maybe we can inquire into a somewhat expansive meaning.

When we look at what is possible in the New Year, we can reflect on our accomplishments and notice some of our failures. We can think about our hopes and our dreams, contributions we made to others, or contributions we wanted to make and didn't. Do we want to forgive someone or ask forgiveness from someone? Who do we want to acknowledge in our lives? In a way, the New Year is really a blank canvas, ready to be filled in during the next 12 months.

Isn't it wonderful to have an opportunity to begin with this newly presented blank canvas? We can create something completely new, a canvas filled with self-expression, possibility and good deeds. We needn't make any excuses. None are necessary.

I'm sure God created this concept of the new year with a deeper meaning. Perhaps the intention is to get closer to our friends and family, ourselves, and certainly to God. This new beginning allows for personal freedom and growth, with some of life's burdens lifted. We can now all begin to fill our personal blank canvas.

Happy New Year /Create abundantly.

Live joyfully/ Enjoy good health.

Embrace/Be happy/Love yourself.

I Go Where The Fish Takes Me

The fish leads me, and I follow.

Whether on land or sea, I go. My yearning unfulfilled. The prize awaits. But for me only? Yes, I must catch you. I must, I must.

The water erupts with high waves, pushing harshly against my face. I pull back, swerving, my catch on my hook.

I stand startled, the not-so-gentle wind at my back. The sweeping water blocking my vision. The boat kneeling. I fear nothing. I'm driven by instinct, focused on my prize. My passion perseveres.

The fish leads me, and I follow. I'm obsessed with the catch, the conquest, the victory. I will stay as long as necessary. When I finish, you will be mine. I will begin again, as I always do.

I am a true fisherman.

Lenore, Lanai, Shamore, Shamai

My daughter told us that she was looking at a house in Florida with a really big Lanai. Growing up in Brooklyn, I never heard of a Lanai. I knew a Lenore; I knew a Lonny and a Lenny.

I only knew of a front porch, a back porch, a back sitting area or a deck. In an apartment building, it's a balcony. Never a Lanai. Now people are talking of how big their Lanai is. How wide it is. Is it screened in? Is it an extended lanai? How much of the Lanai is covered? Everyone needs an extended lanai. Where does it face? The conversation is endless.

A Lanai, by any other name, is still a porch.

I'm picturing what it would be like sitting out in our Lanai. Take a look at our beautiful Lanai.

We are now in the market for a lanai.

The biggest one that we can find. Maybe we will live in our new beautiful Grand Lanai. Our extended, partially covered Lanai will have three bedrooms, a den and 2.5 baths and face a lake.

Our new Lanai will even have a porch, extended, of course.

Look at Me; I See Myself

Look at me; I see myself.

I wonder how others truly see me. As if I can see myself.

Do the eyes see what the heart feels? It can be so lonely.

Can anyone see my history? Can anyone see my essence? Can
anyone see my frailty?

I alone can see the mirror of my soul hidden before the world.

So when you look at me, I see myself.

My Mother, Adela The Saint

I enjoy a loving relationship with my wife Barbara. Our two daughters are awesome, who had a loving relationship with their Nana Adela, my mother, and our two granddaughters have their own Nana Barbara.

I am now becoming aware how much I miss my mother.

There is an emptiness in my heart since my mother, known as Adele, died 12 years ago at age 96.

I was with her when she died, a few days after her 96th birthday. I was going to return to Florida from Brooklyn, NY after being with her for over a week. Her mind was excellent, but her health was failing. I went into her bedroom to be with her.

She said "Norman, are you going home now?" I said "yes, I'm going home soon." She said, "you know, I'm going too." She died about 20 minutes later. She was ready to go. She knew it and said it simply. After her funeral, I left for Florida to continue my life here.

I have now begun to question my sadness about Mom, who was a wonderful human being, with imperfections.

I now have begun to realize the most important things about her, forgiving myself for the way I acted towards my family.

1 remember she offered unconditional love and support, asking for so little in return. My mother was a human being, a saint with flaws.

I didn't understand her love for me.

I remember that I loved cats as a child, rescuing abandoned kittens.

I was a youngster and brought home a half a dozen kittens I found roaming around. Mom said "what are you doing with so many kittens? We don't have the room here for them." I said "they have no home to go to. They are homeless, and they will die if we don't keep them here."

She looked at me and smiled and let me keep those kittens until we found homes for all of them.

I realize my passion and commitment to end homelessness as an adult was probably encouraged from that one incident. She understood what I was saying and my feelings about not abandoning those kittens.

She was always there if needed. All she asked for was a phone call to say hello, how are the kids and grandkids and discuss the weather. That was enough.

Mom was always proud of me whether things were good or bad, since I was her loving son, Norman. I never realized the simplicity and purity of the relationship. I was the one who complicated it miserably, never knowing what she was actually saying to me, wanting me to be independent and make my own decisions.

She had so many qualities of a Saint: kindness, generosity, selflessness, forgiveness, humanity and charity. She took care of me when I was ill as a child. I remember Dr. Karver, who delivered me at birth, and who saved my life when I was 18 months old, suffering from a serious Croup illness. He used to make house calls, and after he examined me, went into the kitchen, filled his pipe, lit it and had a cup of coffee that my mom freshly brewed for him. I still think of Dr. Karver whenever I smell the aroma of a newly lit pipe.

Instead of embracing her generosity and love, I ran away from it. I followed my own personal, solo journey thru life, never realizing my mother was like a Saint. I was the selfish one - she the selfless one.

It took most of my adult life to realize the way a mother loves her child, which was very different from my picture of what it should look like. My expectations and wants from her could never be fulfilled, until I accepted her and myself the way we were, perfectly, imperfect.

I was waiting to be made whole and complete, never accomplishing that. My mother could never give me what I thought I needed. It was not in her power or ability or job to do. I had to find my own path to maturity and wholeness.

She pushed me to be free, like a bird leaving its mother's nest. I had to fly away on my own, creating my own destiny. That was my mother's loving gift to me.

As I continue to write these heartfelt reflections, while still exploring my family history, I am experiencing freedom and gratitude. I love my mother more now. I can now cherish her memory and only ask her forgiveness, and for me to forgive her flaws. Saint Adela, my dear Mother.

Your loving son,

Norman

RANDOM THOUGHTS

The Road

The road to transformation is driven by mediocrity and ignorance.

Being smart doesn't imply nor insure wisdom.

Wisdom comes from a deeper, more spiritual, empathetic place.

A place of being soulful and mindful.

Speaking too much precludes learning and listening.

We can then truly say, I don't know,

I really do not know.

We then begin the road to understanding and transformation.

The question that arises, is transformation so worthwhile?

I tend to assert that it is.

It surely is worth the trip.

Anne Frank

It was so odd and confusing for Anne to even be thinking this way. How could she?

During the last 761 long days and nights being hidden from the Nazis, she was instructed, ordered, pleaded with not to be caught, and just be quiet. Speak in a whisper. Be on your guard every minute of every day. Don't laugh out loud, as if there was ever anything to laugh about. Now, suddenly she had an odd experience of being free, even in the midst of this surreal horror going on around her. If indeed, this new feeling was only for a finite moment of time,

It seemed like a bit of fresh air after those few years of confinement. For Anne, it felt like a prison in the house, behind the wall, with no expected date to be released. Now, she didn't have to just look past the walls, or look at the ceiling, or look at the floor, or look in her mirror. She can, for this moment, look up at the sky. She could touch the air and feel the breeze against her face. There were now people near her, even if they were strangers, other faces that she could look at. She took in their faces, one by one, each unique expression, as they became embedded in her mind and soul. Each new face became a precious possession to Anne.

Yes, this was freedom for her.

Yet, Anne was so confused. What would she have chosen, given the opportunity to be free from the confinement of the two rooms, even though this new, brief experience certainly meant a horrific future?

It was certainly too much for a young girl to even consider. She should not have to be put in this kind of position. She wanted to experience love. She wanted to have new friends. She wanted to experience growing up. She just wanted to experience life as a woman. She was again so angry.

The tears started rolling down her face against her ice-cold cheeks, past her chin, falling finally on the lapel of her very worn and very torn, faded coat. Each tear turning into a little crystal of ice, then slowly melting, lost forever.

She started shaking uncontrollably. She felt so alone and frightened, so isolated, so lost.

So guilty.

She wanted her mama.

Another Thing To Promote

Today, we have something new and exciting to show and promote. Although it may not immediately be for everyone, this is nothing to sneeze at. It's really something great. Please pay close attention.

It's a do-it-yourself home "Get out of my coffin alive survival kit".

Most of us presume that when you're in a coffin you're really dead. However, what if we're not quite so dead? What if we're almost dead but not 100% dead? Is 90% dead really dead enough, when you're in a coffin already? Is 95% acceptable? What about 99% dead? Clearly folks, it's something to seriously think about. Our company thought about it very carefully, and after 5 years of development, our design and technical teams finally came up with this special one-time use survival kit. It consists of a fully charged ready to go cell phone with auto speed dial to 411, 911, 211, 311, and Domino's pizza. Also, a fully charged battery lantern, with a long-life LED bulb, of course. A cutting saw that you can use to easily saw open the coffin. And, we are adding an extra extended expiration dated peanut butter and jelly sandwich on very old white hard crusted bread, for when you get hungry. We're also adding a 10oz. bottle of purified, specialty distilled, mineral added water. For the first hundred people who call in before the show ends, were going to throw in a special newly developed, non-breakable shovel, that comes folded up, and could be opened up to dig yourself out.

Look, I hope you never need it, but who knows; why take a chance? You only live once or so. Operators are now standing by to take all your calls. Please hang up and call back if the phone lines are busy. This special offer won't be around for a long time. It's first come, first served. It's like preparing for a hurricane. You don't want to wait until the winds are a hundred fifty miles an hour for you to go out and buy a generator or run out and buy plywood to board up your windows, or go to the store to fill up your refrigerator, do you? Of course not. We are very pleased to offer this drop-dead one-time price of $4999.99, plus tax and shipping and handling. We will even add, at no additional cost, up to three personalized initials on each of the included items. This is a way for you to say, "this is my special survival kit." Hey, it's a once-in-a-lifetime purchase.

Unfortunately, we have to sell this special promotion "Get out of my coffin alive survival kit" under a no return policy. We are sure you fully understand this policy. Cash or money order or certified checks are only accepted. We are certain that once you use the kit, you will absolutely love it and want to recommend it to everyone you know.

Our operators are standing by now.

Wait a minute folks! A caller is on the line begging to speak to us.

Folks, it's Donald Trump.

"Hello Mr. Trump.

You want to buy one of our kits?

Great. We are so pleased. What?

No, Mr. Trump. It's not a "get out of jail survival kit".

It's a "get out of my coffin alive survival kit".

Oh, you still want to buy one. Oh, 2 kits, Oh, 10 kits, Oh, 20 kits.

You say you never know. You think that they can probably be refitted, and you have many friends and family who might need the kits.

"No, Mr. Trump. You must pay shipping and handling.

No, Mr. Trump, you must pay tax on the kits.

I'm sorry, we can't take a resale tax id number and bill your golf club.

I'm sorry, we can't back date the billing to before the election.

Mr. Trump, is Jared standing there with you?

It seems like questions that he would be asking. No, Mr. Trump. No discounts for multiple orders. Please

Mr. Trump, we have other callers waiting to order,

OK, I 'II put someone on to take your order. Use the kits well and let us know how it goes.

Remember, no returns, if they don't work."

Remember everyone, not suitable for cremations

.

Nothing

Let's promote nothing.

There is no storing nothing, no losing it and no replacing it. It can be the easiest gift you can give anyone, which is nothing. It's very easy to gift nothing as many times as you want.

You never have to worry about nothing breaking and feeling upset about it.

So surely, everyone should line up for nothing.

Why give something if you can give nothing? Isn't it great to never have to worry about a gift to give anybody?. You're always giving them nothing.

No 800 number to call to order nothing.

No worries about supplies of stock of nothing, since there's no inventory or delivery.

No layaway plans available.

You can't return nothing, so there are no issues with customer service.

Wondering how nothing looks? Use your imagination. Nothing can look like anything since you can't think of nothing.

Prices of nothing to be determined. It will, of course, be nothing. You save nothing.

So much time spent on nothing!

Oreo Cookies, An Unacceptable Loss

I just realized that Oreos, my favorite cookie of all time, bar none, now has a racist reference. I have a 75-year relationship with this magnificent cookie.

Now the relationship might be changed forever.

I'm all for changing the names of confederate flags and statues. They represent a horrible part of our American history and should be abolished.

Even my "Aunt Jemima" is affected. I will sadly miss her, along with sweet "Uncle Ben."

Buttttt, Oh my.... my Oreos! Not my Oreos!
l just can't do it! I just can't.
My memories of dunking three or four lovely, sweet, cocoa-rich, sugary, creme-filled Oreos in a glass of delicious, ice-cold whole milk, and mixing it up to make a "mishmash", is too dear a memory to give up. I still savor the process, even now, of the Oreos breaking up and mixing together with the milk, becoming a rich, savory concoction. I took a spoon and then gobbled up the whole glass of this delicious mixture, spoon after spoon, letting it melt in my mouth. The taste and flavor is and was unforgettable.

I'm a bit distraught thinking of not enjoying my dear favorite Oreo cookies ever again. But wait ...
What if I eat fewer Oreos at one time? That's not too bad.

Maybe buy the thin Oreos?

Then, I'm eating less, so maybe it's less racist.

The stigma of the racist reference in the Oreo name may diminish greatly.

Maybe I can eat fewer pancakes. Maybe less Uncle Ben's rice.
Yes...Yes...Yes... the possibilities are endless. My dear Oreos can still be with me.

I feel rejuvenated, more alive!
So, maybe less racism is ok, perhaps more acceptable.
I can be partly racist. And probably thinner! Wow!

Please

Please indulge my unconventional prose without judging me harshly or being overly critical.

I don't write like My Fair Lady, "Wouldn't it be loverly."

I don't write like Mary Poppins, "Remember that a spoon full of sugar makes the medicine go down."

I tend to write to deal with my mortality and fears related to the process.

I like to write about historical events, some with humor, some not.

I try to add a bit of optimism and possibility to my writing, although it may be cloaked with darkness and some morbidity.

Maybe I'm still in the middle ages. I do enjoy a bit of Chaucer's work. I apologize if I interrupt your interest in more happy subjects.

We can all express life's events and address darkness with a bit of humor.

Thank you, and I hope you enjoyed the book.